IMAGES
of America

ROCKAWAY BEACH

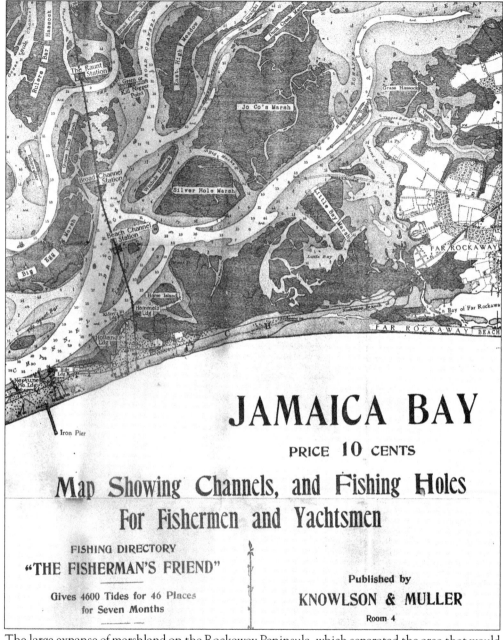

JAMAICA BAY

PRICE 10 CENTS

Map Showing Channels, and Fishing Holes
For Fishermen and Yachtsmen

FISHING DIRECTORY
"THE FISHERMAN'S FRIEND"

Gives 4600 Tides for 46 Places
for Seven Months

Published by
KNOWLSON & MULLER
Room 4

The large expanse of marshland on the Rockaway Peninsula, which separated the area that would become known as Rockaway Beach from the more established community of Far Rockaway to the east, is shown in this turn-of-the-century map. A railroad line and one crude sand road, known today as Rockaway Beach Boulevard, were the only connections between these two portions of the peninsula. (Courtesy of the *Wave*.)

ON THE COVER: A corps of lifeguards, employed by the Queens Borough president, is pictured around 1927 at Rockaway Beach. The borough president's corps was phased out after the city's parks department established its own lifeguard patrol in the late 1920s. (Courtesy of the *Wave*.)

IMAGES
of America

ROCKAWAY BEACH

Vivian Rattay Carter

ARCADIA
PUBLISHING

Published by Arcadia Publishing
Charleston, South Carolina

Library of Congress Control Number: 2011939988

For all general information, please contact Arcadia Publishing:
Telephone 843-853-2070
Fax 843-853-0044
E-mail sales@arcadiapublishing.com
For customer service and orders:
Toll-Free 1-888-313-2665

Visit us on the Internet at www.arcadiapublishing.com

*To Fannie Brush Holland, mother of Rockaway Beach.
Your story of strength and courage inspires me today.*

CONTENTS

ACKNOWLEDGMENTS

The idea to create this book occurred to me in 2008, when I discovered the historical archives of the First Congregational Church of Rockaway Beach. I had read the historical columns of Emil R. Lucev Sr. that had been published in Rockaway's community newspaper, the *Wave*, and enjoyed looking at websites that extolled the glory days of the Rockaway Peninsula. Not much of this material, however, originated from the perspective of present-day residents, so I sensed that I could provide a useful contribution. The story of the people of Rockaway Beach is rich and colorful, yet there are only a handful of published photograph collections about the area. These collections mainly document amusements, hotels, beach scenes, and train and boat services. The social history of year-round residents of the village inside the resort, which filled three-quarters of the calendar year for over a century, had been almost completely ignored.

I therefore needed to tap the expertise of many local history buffs. The people whose efforts laid the foundation for this book include Emil R. Lucev Sr., Ed Gloeggler, Marie E. Velardi, Dean Georges, Ed Sullivan and Dorothy (Auer) Sullivan, Dotsy (Livingston) Kearns, Steve Stathis, and Rosemary (Werner) Tighe. Thank you all, from the bottom of my heart.

Thanks also goes to the following: my Arcadia Publishing acquisitions editor, Erin Vosgien, and production editor, Tim Sumerel; Christina Benson of New York City Parks photo archive; staff of the New York City Municipal archives; Erik Huber of the Long Island Division of Queens Borough Public Library; and Carey Stumm of the New York City Transit Museum. I am also grateful to Susan Locke, Sandy Bernstein, and Howard Schwach of the *Wave* for giving me access to the newspaper's archives and office equipment, and to First Congregational Church of Rockaway Beach. These two sources provided over half the photographs in this book. Unless otherwise noted, all images appear courtesy of the *Wave*, and those provided by the church are credited simply as "FCC."

Friends and family members provided much support—including John Carter, Rebekkah Rodriguez–Thompson, Claire and Evelyn Walsh, Nancy Richman, Sophia Skeans, Joe Manello, Jim Divilly, Noreen Ellis, and Don Riepe. Finally, I thank my parents, Anna Marie Banner and Martin Frank Rattay, for passing on to me their love of nature and history.

INTRODUCTION

In the early 1850s, Capt. Louis Dodge and his wife, Rhoda, arrived by boat and settled in a small cottage on the western portion of the Rockaway Peninsula. At the time, the peninsula was a narrow, wild, and sand-swept strip of land, covered by dunes, marshes, streams, and other wetlands. One crude sand path ran into the area from the east, and the bay and ocean frequently met during high tides and storms. The area was known as "the lower beach," "Rockaway Beach," or simply "the beach," to distinguish it from Far Rockaway, the more developed eastern portion of the peninsula. Far Rockaway had first been settled by Europeans in 1690, and regular stagecoach runs began before the War of 1812. Early land deeds show the entire peninsula as an unincorporated part of the Village of Hempstead (then in Queens County, not Nassau—and not yet a part of New York City). According to the 1860 census, Far Rockaway had over 2,000 year-round residents, and its fashionable Marine Pavilion had been drawing wealthy and famous summer visitors to Rockaway's shore for three decades.

Settlers had shunned the land west of Jarvis Lane, which is today's Beach 9 Street. Even Native American tribes did not reside there, and it is called simply the "Sand Hills" on pre-Colonial maps. It is estimated that just a dozen fishermen's huts were located west of Far Rockaway by 1855. A pond with eel pots graced the Beach 90 Street site, where the *Wave* newspaper now resides, and the dunes covering the area were 30 to 50 feet high. A pioneer named "Aunt" Abby Ryder ran a little clam-chowder house on the shore of Jamaica Bay, near today's Beach 88 Street, and catered to fishermen.

All of this was about to change, as land acquisitions brought more pioneers to the beach by boat or by wagon. The railroad was soon to follow. Captain Dodge was representative of the subsistence fishermen who came seeking a day's catch for the marketplace, plus enough to feed their families. Adventurers and speculators also showed up, eager to get rich and replicate the tourism success of Far Rockaway.

Meanwhile, in 1853 and 1855, James S. Remsen and a partner had purchased large swaths of undeveloped land near today's Beach 102 Street, and the area was soon dubbed "Seaside." The partners established a simple chowder house in a building on the bay soon to be known as the legendary Seaside Hotel, which would spawn other hotels and amusements in the years prior to 1880. In the early 1870s, William Wainwright joined Remsen in the partnership, and Edgar Morrison opened major Seaside ventures in the 1880s. Aunt Abby Ryder's place would ultimately pass to Ryder's daughter Matilda and her husband, Garrett Eldert—becoming a hotel, restaurant, and dock called Eldert's Grove. In the late 1860s, Louis Hammel leased that property and also acquired the land adjoining it. The area between Beach 79 and Beach 88 Streets would come to be known as the "Hammels" section.

Perhaps most significant to the future of the community was the arrival of one prosperous landowning couple with a brood of young children in tow. On April 29, 1858, the schooner *Virginia* landed at a central point of the peninsula near today's Beach 90 Street, bringing the area's newest landowners, Michael and Fannie Holland, who already owned a tobacco business and hotel in Jamaica, Queens. The Hollands had invested $350 to purchase 65 acres of land from Beach 90 to Beach 94 Street, including a small hotel, which they would soon begin operating as a modest tourist lodge called the Holland House, or the Holland Hotel.

The Hollands trucked loads of topsoil from Far Rockaway to turn the dunes into arable land, which could be farmed to provide food for their hotel guests. The Holland farm occupied both sides of Rockaway Beach Boulevard, from Beach 91 to Beach 94 Streets. They also renovated the hotel they had purchased. The following year, Michael Holland died, leaving Fannie Holland to run the business and raise nine children alone. She seemed determined to stay and to make sure that the developing small-town resort became a civilized place. From the outset, it must have looked like the chances of succeeding with this endeavor were questionable. The oldest Holland child, Thomas, was just 15 at the time.

Succeed Fannie Holland did. The value of the Hollands' $350 investment grew to over $1 million within 50 years. The success of these settlers would soon attract other entrepreneurs in the building trades to the peninsula, and together, they built much that appealed to summer visitors, including a mechanical museum that was described as an advanced marvel for its time. There were dance halls, saloons, bathhouses, and restaurants with picnic groves shaded by cedar trees, which had dotted the peninsula when the settlers arrived. There were inns, cottages, and hotels, both small and large. The Holland Hotel had just 25 rooms and was completely rebuilt in 1877. A tourism guide of the era describes it as "strictly a family hotel, of the quietest, neatest, most comfortable character . . . Mrs. Holland, the matronly owner, manages everything personally, and every guest receives particular attention and good care."

These early pioneers attended to the creation of transportation infrastructure, which was needed to bring hordes of tourists to their establishments. They extended five long piers into Jamaica Bay so that steamships and other large vessels could deposit passengers, who had boarded at points in Canarsie, Brooklyn, Manhattan, and even Newark, New Jersey. In fact, so many visitors arrived by boat or train that Rockaway Beach could be considered the model of one of the earliest walker-friendly resort communities—provided one was careful of those trains and trolleys, which regularly dealt death and injury to the unwary.

Although bicycles became a craze in the late 1890s, elsewhere in the city—notably in Far Rockaway—the relatively primitive condition of the streets at the beach and the swarming throngs of pedestrians that overtook the walkways no doubt inhibited the presence of bicyclists. Evidence of their presence during that era is a photograph of a lone bicyclist standing near a sign at the Atlantic Park Hotel on the fringes of Arverne, which tried to attract them by billing itself as "the wheelman's rest" at the beach. There is also an image of a lone rider pedaling along a parade route and another of a bicycle parked near the police station.

Instead, trains and boats were the preferred mode of transportation. In 1872, the train line from Far Rockaway was extended to Rockaway Beach on a track running along the ocean. In 1879, the iconic Iron Pier opened. Built in hopes of creating a bustling landing for millions of visitors, it was a 32-foot-wide esplanade extending 1,300 feet into the Atlantic Ocean near Beach 105 Street. In August 1880, the New York, Woodhaven, and Rockaway Railroad opened its five-mile link to the area, carrying 65,000 passengers on the first day. This second rail line ran along the bay side. The earliest maps indicate the five bay front landings—Hammels, Eldert's, Holland's, Seaside, and Neptune House, near the terminus of the train lines at today's Beach 108 Street.

In August 1881, there was a brief opening of the Rockaway Beach Hotel, dubbed "the Imperial" by its proprietors. Together with its bathhouse, the Rockaway Beach Hotel filled almost seven blocks of beachfront on the fringes of Seaside from Beach 112 to Beach 119 Streets, making it the largest hotel in the world at the time. The hotel did not thrive, though, and was dismantled eight years later. This all occurred before the Village of Rockaway Beach was even a part of New York City.

In the waning years of the 19th century, known as the Progressive era, civic activism blossomed. In 1897, the Hammels, Holland, and Seaside sections combined to form the Village of Rockaway

Beach, although the area was still often referred to by its post office name, Oceanus, for decades. These pioneers at the shore had established a self-reliant small town, tucked away inside a bustling seasonal resort. Residents had not only built the commercial infrastructure of a thriving resort serving millions of tourists a year, they had also constructed houses of worship, schools, and fraternal halls, volunteer fire companies, civic associations, yacht clubs, athletic leagues, choirs, and drama societies—all of which operated year-round. By 1915, there was the Rockaway Park Citizens' Association, Rockaway Beach Citizens' Lighting Committee, Property Owners of Rockaway Beach, Atlantic Athletic Association, Fraternal Order of Eagles, German-American Arion Musical Societies, St. Monica Society of St. Rose of Lima, the DeSales Players, Altar Society of St. Camillus Church, Ladies' Aid of First Congregational Church, the Democratic Club of the Fifth Ward, Oceanus Dramatic League, Frank L.A. O'Connor Players, a Woman's Suffrage Association, the Bay Side Fishing Club, and many other private boating organizations.

These community groups were locally oriented escapes from the wild gaiety at seasonal businesses that were serving masses of visitors. Residents, who had no doubt worked long hours in their tourism businesses during the busy season from May to September, relaxed with gusto in the off-season. Just a peek at issues of the *Wave* documents that regular dinners, fundraising auctions, card parties, athletic contests, concerts, and variety shows were being offered at the beach, even on weeknights in the first week of January. The front page of the January 1915 *Wave* says that during one event, a long evening of dinner and dancing concluded "in the wee hours of Tuesday morning"—and the Roaring Twenties hadn't even started yet.

After the failure of the mammoth hotel, the area would never aspire to be associated, like other beach resorts, with huge hotels and casinos. Millions of visitors still came, but the existing hotels could not accommodate all of them. By the turn of the century, a modest and simple innovation—casual summer housing in huge tent and bungalow colonies—would be the biggest boon of all for the resort of Rockaway Beach. This was the defining seasonal housing remembered by generations of summer visitors to the peninsula; however, there were other changes in store.

By the peak of the maritime era in the late 1890s, the City of New York decided to acquire Jamaica Bay and adjacent land, including the newborn Village of Rockaway Beach. The intention was to fold it into the new Borough of Queens and create a hub for future ship-based commerce. In 1917, Albert H. Bellot published the *History of the Rockaways*. The charming little booklet unabashedly boosts the success story of Rockaway Beach, noting all the community organizations and services that had been established. The book also points out that trains to and from Manhattan run every 30 minutes, steamships and ferries ply the waters, and trolley service is also available almost from end to end across the peninsula. Bellot also describes how residents of the peninsula have been fighting to get out from under the city's umbrella since 1910, finding state assembly support for three separate secession bills in 1915, 1916, and 1917. All three times, New York City's "boy mayor," John Purroy Mitchel (who had been elected at age 34), dashed local hopes by vetoing the bills.

It would take 40 years, but each item on the list of secessionists' demands was eventually satisfied by the city, including new bridges and roadways, a new boardwalk, and an up-to-date sewer system. The resort and the village thrived. By the summer of 1950, the pinnacle of success had been achieved, with 48 million visitors tallied for that season. Despite this, there seemed to be an implicit price set by the city in exchange for meeting residents' demands for improved services. In return, from the mid-1950s through the mid-1960s, the city sited the vast bulk of federally subsidized, low- and middle-income housing projects in Queens on the Rockaway Peninsula, in some cases razing popular amusements and tent or bungalow colonies in order to build these high-rise projects. Even more devastating, the loss of Long Island Rail Road service due to a trestle fire in May 1950 crippled the Rockaway Beach community for six years. The area never recovered from this shock.

If there were ever a symbolic trio of major events announcing an area's decline, the loss of a hospital, school, and courthouse all within the space of four years would have to be one, and this is precisely what happened to Rockaway Beach from 1959 to 1962. The Rockaway Beach Hospital was put up for sale in late 1959, after the Peninsula Hospital opened in Arverne. The aged, but architecturally distinguished, Public School 44 was demolished in 1960 and replaced by the boxy and pedestrian Public School 183 building on Beach 79 Street in 1960. Finally, the Rockaway Beach courthouse, which had been contemplated by its Depression-era planners as a grand entrance point for the peninsula and a shining symbol of civic pride, was closed due to "citywide court consolidation" in 1962. The building was not torn down and sold for scrap, much like the mammoth Rockaway Beach Hotel, but left in place, boarded up, and trussed in scaffolding as a stark, constant reminder of civic decline. While these devastating social transformations were progressing, much like dominoes falling in a row, the seeds of the neighborhood's present-day rejuvenation were just beginning to bear fruit.

That rejuvenation would come from surfing. After decades during which visitors to the beach seemed to demand wild amusements with no holds barred, the focus was once again on being in the water and close to the sea. The designation of New York City's first surfing-only beach in 2005 gave Rockaway Beach an enormous boost. With little seasonal housing and virtually no hotels, day visitors were just about the only visitors, and surfers began coming to Rockaway for the day. It was clear that new food options close to the surfing beach had a great chance for success.

Within a few years, a group of hip, new snack shacks opened up in Rockaway Beach on the border of the old Playland Amusement Park site. Modeled on the bodega taquerias of Brooklyn's Sunset Park, the soccer field grill scene in Red Hook, and a touch of added Baja California style, these cafés quickly attracted long lines of foodies with smart phones. A group, headed up by David Selig, successfully acquired the boardwalk food concession contract from the New York City Parks Department in 2010.

Meanwhile, residents have lobbied for improved transportation, recreation, and schools, both to attract visitors and improve their own employment options and quality of life. Churches, which once formed a major pillar of community stability, strive to retain members and maintain their relevance in today's world of instant electronic communications.

Business district improvement is high on the agenda of local concerns. Many hope that Rockaway Beach will again become a widely popular resort and that all will share in its prosperity. They also strive to understand why social services operations continue to find the peninsula more attractive than retail and tourism businesses, and elected officials seem unable to reverse the trend.

Some residents would love to see the self-reliant, walker-friendly village of Rockaway Beach make a return, complete with bungalows and open-air tent colonies, small family inns serving clam chowder and craft beers surrounded by cedar picnic groves and vegetable gardens, ferries regularly plying the waters, and a suburban-style train line making a trip to Penn Station in 30 minutes. For now, it's just a dream.

One

PIONEERS AT THE SHORE
1850s–1920s

In the early 1850s, Rockaway Beach was a wild, marshy, windswept, mostly deserted place. The earliest settlers lived in fishermen's huts, and chowder houses were the first restaurants. Within 30 years, the community had grown into a wildly popular resort served by a thriving rail line. Amusement parks, hotels, taverns, and dance halls abounded. The wealthy still summered in Far Rockaway, and the lower-class thronged the beaches of Coney Island, which could be reached with a nickel fare. A dime or more was needed to get to Rockaway Beach on a train or a boat, so the resort attracted solid middle-class visitors.

The settlers were building a seasonal resort, but by 1897, when the Hammel, Holland, and Seaside sections combined to form the Village of Rockaway Beach, they had also built a civilized and self-sufficient year-round community. Included in this community were houses of worship, schools and fraternal halls, volunteer fire companies, civic associations, yacht clubs, choirs, and drama societies.

The village lost its independence a year later, when the City of New York acquired the Rockaway Peninsula and incorporated it into the new Borough of Queens. Within a decade, the residents of Rockaway Beach, along with the rest of the peninsula, determined that the union had not been beneficial to them and commenced years dedicated to efforts to secede.

Although the secession effort was ultimately abandoned in 1917 after three successive mayoral vetoes, these civic efforts bore other fruit. Citizens of Rockaway Beach had mobilized to build their own free hospital and dispensary, formally dedicated upon final completion in 1915. In 1922, they built the Rockaway Beach National Bank, and soon, their lobbying efforts would result in a bridge providing a direct connection to the mainland for automobiles. Despite all of this development, there were still many open fields and houses surrounded by scenic groves of trees in their little village.

In 1877, John Jamieson and John Bond founded the Jamieson & Bond Company in a two-story building located on the bay at Bond Avenue (today's Beach 96 Street). An advertisement for their business appeared in Alfred Bellot's 1917 *History of the Rockaways* and listed the company's products as "ice, coal, wood, mason materials, hay and feed, cement building blocks, and roofing slag." The Jamieson and Bond families lived side by side in homes at nos. 9 and 11 on North Bond Avenue. The photograph above shows the building under construction, and below is the finished edifice. (Both, courtesy of FCC.)

This early view of the company's employees (above) probably dates to the 1880s or 1890s. Bond wears a suit, in the second row and third from left. Jamieson is seated in the first row, far right, wearing overalls and a hat. Employees in the front row hold feathered tools used to clean chimney flues. A rare interior view of the office at Jamieson & Bond (below) is from the same time period. (Both, courtesy of FCC.)

Alfred Curtis Bedell, a railroad carpenter with a strong interest in architecture, moved with his family to Rockaway Beach in 1877. Bedell poses for this 1879 portrait with wife, Georgianna, and his daughters Araminta (left) and Celestia. In the 1880s and 1890s, the Bedell offspring were friends with Fannie Holland's many grandchildren. (Courtesy of Marie E. Velardi.)

John Bond and Alfred Bedell would join together in 1881 to organize a Protestant Sabbath School, or Sunday school, for the children living at the beach. The classes were held in the home of Fannie Holland, and the families of students would eventually become the founders of the First Congregational Church. Their names are listed in the church's minute book, with Bedell incorrectly named as Albert instead of Alfred. (Courtesy of FCC.)

At a meeting of the citizens of Rockaway Beach, held at School House, on Sunday afternoon, December 25th 1881, it was found desirable to organize a Sabbath School, on which occasion, the following persons, after being regularly moved and seconded, were duly elected to office: elected by acclamation: Norman Allen, Superintendent; A. B. Smith, Trustee; Albert Bedell, " ; John A. Bond, " ; Miss Bostwick, Vice-Sup't

FIRST CONGREGATIONAL CHURCH
Rockaway Beach, L.I.

In 1886, the families voted to build a church where they could conduct services and Sunday school classes, and decided to affiliate with the Congregationalists. Fannie Holland, a Methodist, donated land at 92-13 Rockaway Beach Boulevard, located just to the east of the present-day Peninsula Library. Bedell drew the architectural plans for the church, which was dedicated in 1888. This is a rare early postcard showing the building at its original site. (Courtesy of FCC.)

In 1886, Seraphina Magliola donated land on Fairview Avenue (today's Beach 84 Street) north of Rockaway Beach Boulevard for the area's first Roman Catholic church, St. Rose of Lima. Note the trolley tracks, which ran across the peninsula by 1897. The present-day Romanesque-style church for the parish, located down the street at the corner of Shorefront Parkway, replaced this modest structure in 1907. (Courtesy of Dean Georges.)

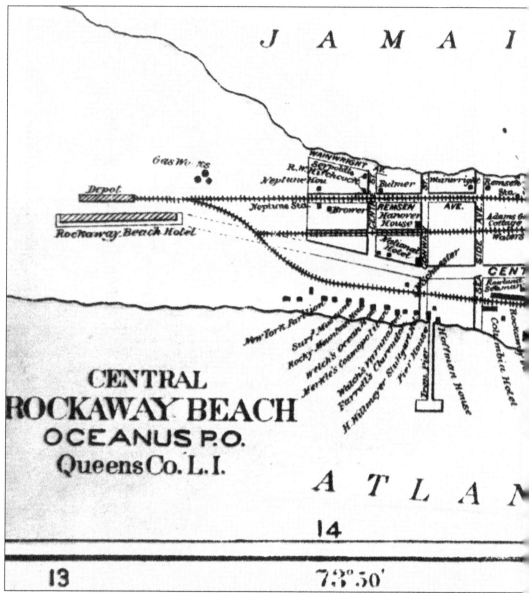

This Beers 1886 map of Rockaway Beach shows locations of early hotels, piers, and train stations. Across from the Holland Hotel is the notation "P.O.M.P. Holland." Fannie Holland's son Michael P. Jr. was the first postmaster of Oceanus and responsible for picking up the mail in Jamaica and bringing it to the beach for distribution. In the days before house-to-house delivery, postmasters

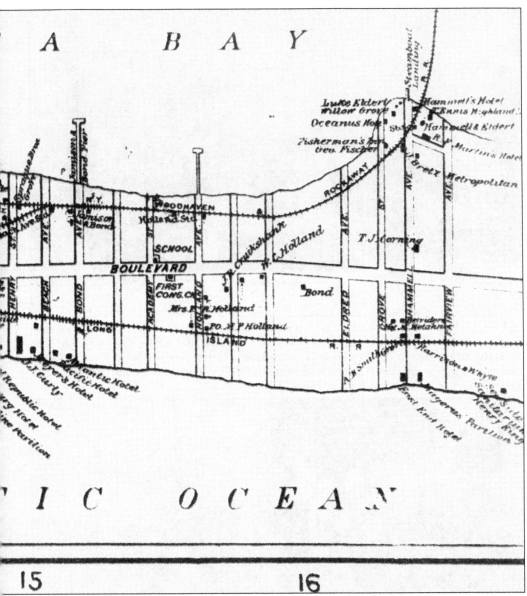

published names in the newspaper as notification that a letter or package had been received. This map shows two separate rail lines at the time, one along the beach and a second along the bay. It also marks locations of stands of trees belonging to the Sprague brothers and E.E. Datz, as well as Adams Grove.

In 1878, Michael P. Jr.'s wife, Julia Holland, was hired by the Town of Hempstead to be Rockaway Beach's first schoolteacher. Classes were held in the Holland and Schmeelk homes. The first schoolhouse was built in 1881 at the site of today's 100th Precinct Station House. Julia conducted classes until she gave birth to her only child, Fannie, in 1883. (Courtesy of Queens Borough Public Library, Long Island Division, Emil R. Lucev Collection.)

Rockaway Beach students are pictured around 1890. In 1878, a visiting writer noted 18 scholars at the school in the Holland home, adding, "the winter census of the beach is about 35 persons, mostly proprietors of the restaurants, who find it economical to occupy their buildings in winter, thereby saving rent for a dwelling in the city." (Courtesy of FCC.)

The resort experienced brisk business in these years; however, there were frequently storms and fires, which destroyed hotels, attractions, and infrastructure, such as piers and landings. The Great Seaside Fire of 1892 was the best known of all, as it leveled several blocks of hotels and amusements. This rare early view shows the fire's destruction.

The Great Seaside Fire of 1892 was not much of a setback to the resort town's continued growth. Within a short period of time, the area was rebuilt, and newspaper stories deemed it to be even better than before. Shown is a postcard view of the new boardwalk between Seaside and Holland, which was completed in 1893.

Some establishments, like the 300-room Seaside House, were built even bigger and grander than they had been before. It was unusual for a building to have more than three floors. This rare photograph of the Seaside House is dated prior to an 1880 renovation that added a fourth story topped by a mansard roof and a small tower. (Courtesy of Queens Borough Public Library, Long Island Division, Illustrations Collection—Rockaways.)

Shortly after Rockaway Beach and Queens County became part of New York City in 1898, the first police station was built on a site just behind the present-day Irish Circle Restaurant on Beach 102 Street and Rockaway Beach Boulevard. The building later became the Crystal Hotel, and the police moved to the old schoolhouse building, which was razed in 1929 to construct the 100th Precinct Station House.

Unfortunately, millions of tourists attracted pickpockets, hustlers, and swindlers. Newspaper accounts document that colorful hotel entrepreneurs, such as E.E. Datz, often took it upon themselves to deal with the criminal element, but a police force was essential. In this photograph (above) in front of Avondale by the Sea, a hotel in the Hammels section, the horse-drawn police wagon is marked "79th Precinct." Policemen in vehicles like these were brought in to restore order in the saloons and the enclosed vehicles came to be known by the derisive ethnic slur "paddy wagons." Below is the Rockaway Beach Police around 1900.

The police force has assembled around 1900 in front of the Seaside Fire House. The legend above the door reads, "Seaside Hose & Engine Co. No. 1, 88 HEC." Early police uniforms had two rows of buttons.

An early constable stands with two police officers around 1900 in front of the old station house. By 1901, according to Bellot's *History of the Rockaways*, the unit was numbered as the 281st Precinct and had a contingent of 52 officers covering a jurisdiction from Arverne to Rockaway Point.

This c. 1890 photograph (above) shows a Rockaway Beach Police parade on Rockaway Beach Boulevard near Beach 88 Street. The caption of this early postcard (right) reads, "Police Squad, Rockaway Beach." The sign above the door notes that it is the 79th Precinct Station House.

Even before the Great Seaside Fire of 1892, when Rockaway was still part of the town of Hempstead, volunteer fire companies were formed to protect property at the beach. In 1886, the Oceanus Hook and Ladder Company No. 1 was established. Its horse-drawn equipment was kept in a shed at the corner of Beach 84 Street and Rockaway Beach Boulevard. The company also stored equipment near the bay at the Hammels Hotel.

Michael P. Holland Jr. and the patriarch of another pioneer family, Rowland J. Seaman, were charter members of the Oceanus Hook and Ladder Company No. 1. This c. 1900 photograph of the volunteer force was taken after they built a new firehouse at Beach 88 Street and Rockaway Beach Boulevard. It housed both the Oceanus Hook and Ladder Company No. 1 and the Oceanus Engine Company No. 2.

Joe Rogers   Hy Holland   Stev OhaAA   Jos. Davis.   Wm G Runner   Hy Repperger   Hy Jamison.

ER. Redden.   Joez Joel   Fred Melohn   Frank Bartle   John Boyd   Jac Rosenkka

Emil Kummens   Perne DeLaun   Wm A Rogers   Geo Ureeland   Lom J McVay   John Whally   Frank Spence

J L McSheHry   Wm Ryder   Wm E Gross   Fred Gelewsky   Martin Gad

Another volunteer fire company in the Hammels area at the turn of the century was Atlantic Hose Company No. 1, located at Beach 86 Street. Portraits of the firefighters were labeled at the time to identify each man. Pioneer families are prominently represented. William A. Rogers, third from the left in the second row from the bottom, was married to John Jamieson's daughter Adelaide.

A third volunteer department was the Seaside Hose and Engine Company No. 1. The firehouse for that group was located on the north side of Rockaway Beach Boulevard between what are today Beach 102 and Beach 103 Streets. This photograph shows the volunteers with their horse-drawn, steam-powered pump and hose equipment.

The Seaside Hose and Engine Company No. 1 (above) poses in front of the Cook Brothers' Milk & Cream Store, located at Beach 102 Street and Rockaway Beach Boulevard. The store enjoyed a degree of celebrity when one of the brothers, Frederick Cook, who had worked as a seasonal milk deliveryman at the beach during his college years, went on the first expedition to the North Pole in 1908. Robert E. Peary is sometimes given credit for reaching the landmark first, but other sources say Peary did not arrive at the North Pole until after Cook, in 1909. Below is a c. 1900 photograph of the fire company with its hoses on display for a parade.

The photograph on the right shows the crowd leaning into the street with anticipation during a demonstration by the hose unit in a parade along Rockaway Beach Boulevard, near Beach 88 Street. Another demonstration with apparatus during the same parade, held in the mid- to late 1890s, is pictured below.

This horse-drawn unit is in the parade. This is one of few early photographs showing a bicyclist in Rockaway Beach. A woman is seen traveling along the street on a two-wheeled conveyance to the left of the parade units, near the streetlight pole.

The Seaside Hose and Engine Company No. 1 is pictured in 1904. A prominent sign behind the company members advertises, "This block for sale in plots to suit." The era was quite an active time for development in the Seaside area, as seasonal housing in tent colonies and bungalows was burgeoning.

Here is another photograph of the Seaside Hose and Engine Company No. 1 in 1904. Trolley tracks can be seen on the street. Trolley service ran along Rockaway Beach Boulevard directly in front of the Seaside engine house from the late 1890s until buses replaced trolleys in 1925.

Volunteer fire companies continued to exist, even after the City of New York established a professional, paid corps of firefighters in 1905. The Oceanus Hook and Ladder Company No. 1 is pictured in 1904, with its firehouse decorated for a holiday celebration. The poster hanging on the building to the right of the men advertises a volunteer firefighters' event in October 1904.

The *Brooklyn Daily Eagle*'s 1907 almanac lists Queens fire companies, including Engine Company 167, headed by Charles F. Connolly, at Rockaway Beach Boulevard and Henry Street (today's Beach 102 Street). This turn-of-the-century photograph shows the company and its equipment. (Courtesy of Edward and Dorothy Auer Sullivan.)

Decorations for patriotic holidays were quite elaborate in Rockaway Beach. To the right in the foreground, a lone bicycle can be seen parked at the curb.

Turn-of-the-century parade photographs, such as the one above, show numerous trees, which were thought to be favorable for business on the peninsula. Early tourist guides describe several Rockaway Beach hotels as having picnic groves. The Beers map (pages 16 and 17) marks the locations of stands of trees belonging to the Sprague brothers and E.E. Datz, as well as Adams Grove. Patriotism and lighthearted fun went hand-in-hand at the volunteer fire companies. Some of the members of this neighboring Arverne fire company, shown below, are dressed in costume, and a young girl seems to be striking a playful pose.

The community outgrew the tiny schoolhouse before long. In 1897, the cornerstone was laid for a grand, new school building at the corner of Academy Avenue and Rockaway Beach Boulevard, the site of today's Peninsula Library. In 1899, when the new Public School 44 was being constructed, the First Congregational Church decided to move its building a block away to a plot of land south of Rockaway Beach Boulevard, between Beach 94 and Beach 95 Streets in an area known today as the site of the Doughboy Memorial. Below is a rare view of the interior of the original church sanctuary, photographed in May 1938 just before the building was demolished to make room for the new city parking field. (Both, courtesy of FCC.)

John R. Corning specialized in moving buildings, and early issues of the *Wave* document that his services were in great demand. The First Congregational Church kept the receipt showing his labor costs, dated November 27, 1899, in its archives. Human laborers were paid in the range of $2.50 a day, while horses cost $1.50 a day. (Courtesy of FCC.)

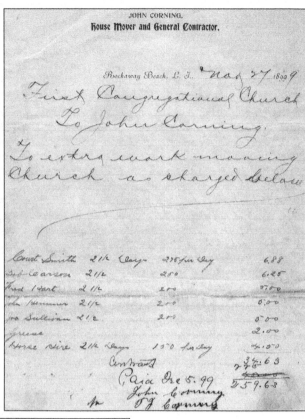

Once the church had moved out of the shadow of the large new school building, a small piece of property remained. It was purchased by Dr. Hilbert B. Tingley, MD, for construction of a medical office. Albert Bedell recalls in his memoirs that the doctor owned the first automobile at the beach. In January 1903, Doctor Tingley was killed while boarding a trolley car. (Courtesy of Queens Borough Public Library, Long Island Division— Portraits Collection.)

By 1893, when Rev. William Kershaw was called as pastor at the First Congregational Church, saloons and hotels were a big part of life at the beach. A few temperance advocates pressured him to preach at prohibition rallies in Seaside. Kershaw refused, saying he did not agree with the movement's premise that consumption of alcohol condemned a person to eternal damnation. In June 1896, he left Rockaway to become a pastor at a Brooklyn church. This is a portrait of Kershaw and his family. (Courtesy of FCC.)

The church called a new pastor, Rev. John C. Green, who would lead them through the mid-1930s, an era of surging membership growth. The church expanded from 50 to 500 members by 1917. A spacious new parsonage was built in 1905 on the south side of Rockaway Beach Boulevard between Beach 94 and Beach 95 Streets, west of the church sanctuary. (Courtesy of FCC.)

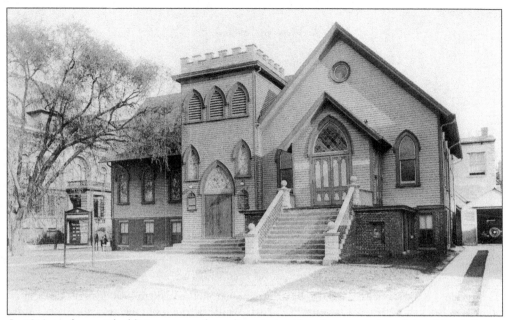

In 1913, a substantial addition was made to the existing church sanctuary, and the old steeple was removed from the roof (above). Visible at the left of the church in this 1913 photograph (below) is the Rockaway Beach Post Office, which moved several times over the years until it landed at its present 90-12 Rockaway Beach Boulevard location, formerly the site of Arion Hall. In addition to managing the family's real estate holdings, which were significant, Michael P. Holland Jr. served as postmaster in 1882. The community's post office address was Oceanus, a name that James Remsen had given to the neighborhood in the 1870s. (Both, courtesy of FCC.)

This receipt for 300 service cards ordered by the church from the *Wave* in 1901 gives the newspaper's address as Rockaway Beach, Oceanus P.O., Fifth Ward, Borough of Queens, New York. Fannie Holland died in June 1893. Her son William C. and his wife, Margaret (Brower) Holland, were the parents of 13 children by the 1890 census. William had apprenticed with tea and coffee merchants in Manhattan at the age of 14, and by 1891, he ran a leading local grocery outfit, W.C. Holland & Son, on 86-02 Rockaway Beach Boulevard. William and Margaret Holland's brood is pictured below around 1905. (Above, courtesy of FCC; below, courtesy of Marie E. Velardi and Jim Pearsall.)

The interiors of these two early-20th-century stores in Rockaway Beach are typical of what would have been seen inside the Holland grocery establishment. According to Alfred J. Bedell's memoir of early life in Rockaway Beach, William Holland's son Charles got a job maintaining the kerosene streetlamps of the village in the 1890s, and the young boys would often tag along to help, fascinated with the donkey cart Holland used to carry his supplies.

Having enjoyed the right to run for office and vote in their church governing body since 1886, female members of the First Congregational Church were in the forefront of the movement for women's suffrage. In these two c. 1910 photographs, the distinctive white dresses associated with the suffrage movement are seen, and Cora Babcock (above, third row, third from left) assertively hoists the flag. Women would win the right to vote in US elections in January 1920. Others pictured include John Jamieson (first row, center, holding his daughter Constance), Rev. John C. Green (to the left of Jamieson), and Michael P. Holland Jr. (to the right of Jamieson). The First Congregational Church Sunday school students (below) sport bonnets, ribbons, and even tricornered hats. (Both, courtesy of FCC.)

Pictured above is the first confirmation class of the First Congregational Church in 1909. From left to right are (first row) Arthur Reppinger, George Wagner, Adolph H. Knoll Jr., and Richard Roland; (second row) unidentified, Dora Schafer, Mabel Holland, Gladys Wheelwright, Rev. John C. Green, Helen Schafer, Laura Holland, Anna Freely, and Wina Wheelwright; (third row) Susan Galke, Alice Wheelwright, Louise Bossard, unidentified, Ruth George, ? Wheelwright, Helen Bullwinkle, Helen Bell, and Helen Sendeker. There are probably adults named Wheelwright, Schafer, and Holland in attendance at this adult education program held in the auditorium of Public School 44 in this 1909 photograph below. (Above, courtesy of FCC; below, courtesy of NYC Municipal Archives.)

This is an early-20th-century portrait of a child, thought to be John Jamieson's daughter Ella, baptized at the First Congregational Church. She later married Edward Zimmerman and lived in the brick bungalow at 320 Beach 98 Street until 1958. (Courtesy of FCC.)

Alfred J. Bedell, son of the original architect of the church, Alfred Curtis, grew up with the children and grandchildren of the Holland family. He married Adelaide Sprague on February 13, 1907. Sprague was photographed around the date of the marriage at Rockaway Beach in her winter finery. (Courtesy of Marie E. Velardi.)

Rose Werner was an active volunteer with the First Congregational Church Sunday School. She is pictured in 1908 with her infant son William. (Courtesy of Rosemary Werner Tighe.)

William Werner is pictured modeling his winter coat and hat. He would go on to practice medicine at the Rockaway Beach Hospital and Dispensary, pioneering the use of hypnotism in lieu of anesthesia during labor and delivery in the 1950s, before the Lamaze method was introduced in the United States. The idea had been suggested to Werner by one of his prenatal patients. (Courtesy of Rosemary Werner Tighe.)

The community banded together to obtain a local hospital of its own. In 1908, a charter was received and fundraising began in earnest to pay for a structure. Pictured is the Rockaway Beach Hospital after its dedication in 1915. The first patient was received in 1911, after one wing was completed and the facility had just 37 beds. A three-story brick extension was added in 1924. (Courtesy of Ed Gloeggler.)

By the time the hospital opened, Public School 44's enrollment was growing larger, as seen in this photograph of the 1917 graduating class. Youngsters helped raise funds in various ways. Girls collected flowers throughout the neighborhood to sell at a booth, and a contest was held to select a contingent of 300 attractive young women, deputized en masse to collect loose change from beachgoers in support of the hospital fund.

John Jamieson was an original board member of Rockaway Beach Hospital. Tragically, his nephew David, 19, drowned in the surf near Beach 98 Street along with John Bond's son Bruce, 21, in December 1910. The two had joined with a group of other young men to establish an Oceanus lifesaving station, and perished during the second test of their 18-foot Seabright skiff when it was capsized by a 20-foot wave. This is an early photograph of boatbuilding at the beach. (Courtesy of FCC.)

Called to the scene of the waterfront tragedy was an ambulance from St. Joseph's Hospital in Far Rockaway. The Rockaway Beach Hospital would obtain its own ambulance years later, and board members have gathered here to mark the happy occasion. The hospital's charter specified that the board was to include 15 members—"five Protestants, five Hebrews and five Catholics."

John Jamieson generously donated or sold his land to benefit the church and the wider community on more than one occasion. This is an early-1920s view of a ground-breaking, probably for the Rockaway Beach National Bank. Jamieson, sporting his trademark mustache, is at right center with his foot on the shovel. (Courtesy of FCC.)

The Rockaway Beach National Bank opened for business in 1922 in this grand, classical structure at the northwest corner of Beach 95 Street and Rockaway Beach Boulevard. The sign announces, "Your Home Town Bank. Open Saturday evening, 7–9 p.m." Trolley tracks are visible on the street in front, while a rustic Jamieson & Bond outbuilding is at back. (Courtesy of Ed Gloeggler.)

The community now had its own school, hospital, bank, and four houses of worship. By 1925, it would also have a bridge providing a direct connection to the mainland for automobiles. The bridge can be seen in the distance in this photograph of Beach 95 Street facing the bay. Despite all of this development, there were still many open fields and houses surrounded by farmland and scenic groves of trees. (Courtesy of Queens Borough Public Library, Long Island Division, Emil R. Lucev Collection.)

Two

VILLAGE INSIDE A BUSTLING RESORT
1920s–1940s

By the early 1920s, residents of Rockaway Beach had established thriving and essential local institutions and services. By 1925, Rockaway Beach would also have a bridge providing a direct connection to the mainland for automobiles. Better roadways and bridges had been a key demand of the secession movement. Residents had also asked for a new boardwalk extending all the way from Far Rockaway to Neponsit and an up-to-date sewer system; nobody, however, asked for high-rise housing.

This squeaky wheel at the beach would eventually get the city's attention, most notably with a brand-new boardwalk in 1929. The homegrown ideas and plans generated by the civic leaders of Rockaway Beach would eventually have to contend with the ideas and plans of more distant power brokers. In 1922, youthful Queens borough president Maurice Connolly commissioned artists' renderings of 14-story high-rises and roadways along the shore in Rockaway Beach. These drawings would later inspire Robert Moses, who dominated the reconstruction of the parks, transportation, and housing infrastructure of New York City for three decades during the 1930s, 1940s, and 1950s. Under Moses's direction, Rockaway Beach, along with the entire peninsula, would eventually get many of those high-rises and roadways. The resilient people and institutions of the community adapted as necessary to accommodate these improvements. Churches and schools moved, and proprietors of seasonal businesses sometimes had to pull up stakes and relocate.

Unfortunately for Rockaway Beach, the City of New York looked disparagingly on tent and bungalow colonies with open-air courtyards. These casual, decidedly low-rise summer housing options had drawn middle-class families from the early 1900s through the 1940s. The most popular attractions of the beach and boardwalk, such as roller coasters, Ferris wheels, carnival games, and snack stands, were also considered "cheap amusements" by Moses. The texture of Rockaway Beach as a resort was largely swept away during Moses's tenure. The residents, and their vibrant, year-round community, served by a suburban-style train line and numerous seasonal waterborne transportation options, continued to thrive into the 1950s.

In December 1927, the Holland and Hammels sections of Rockaway Beach still has the feel of a small village. Side streets in the neighborhood, like Beach 79 Street, remain unpaved. (Courtesy of Len Kohn.)

The Rockaway secession movement, which began in 1910 and continued through 1917, had demanded better roadways and the construction of a highway across the peninsula; however, in 1927, Beach 88 Street is still a tree-lined, rutted road. (Courtesy of Len Kohn.)

Beach 90 Street has expansive open spaces in November 1927, with wide berth for the few motor vehicles about, such as the car in the right foreground advertising the Edgemere Nash dealership. Buses had superseded trolleys by 1925 along Rockaway Beach Boulevard, replacing one type of congestion on that main street with another. (Courtesy of Len Kohn.)

Beach 91 Street was, at the time, the location of the Holland Train Station, located just past the dark picket fence on the right. On the left behind the trees is the McKennee Building on Rockaway Beach Boulevard, which, by the time of this November 1927 photograph, housed the public library for Rockaway Beach. Today, elected officials and physicians occupy the building's suites. (Courtesy of Len Kohn.)

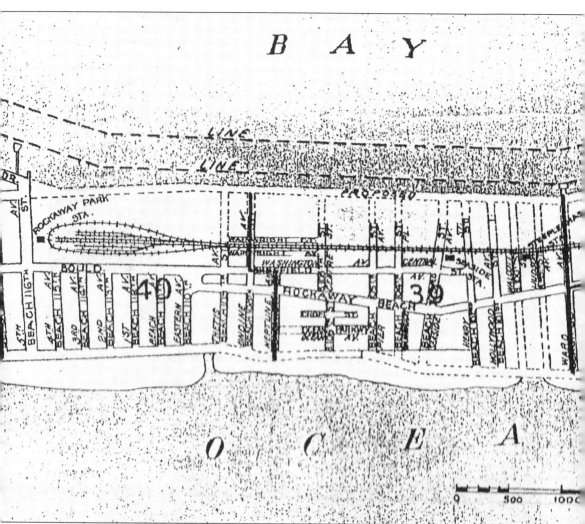

Although the city was slow to harness the resources to pave many of its side streets, it did decide to rename them in February 1916. This map, published by the Ullitz Company in 1919, was no

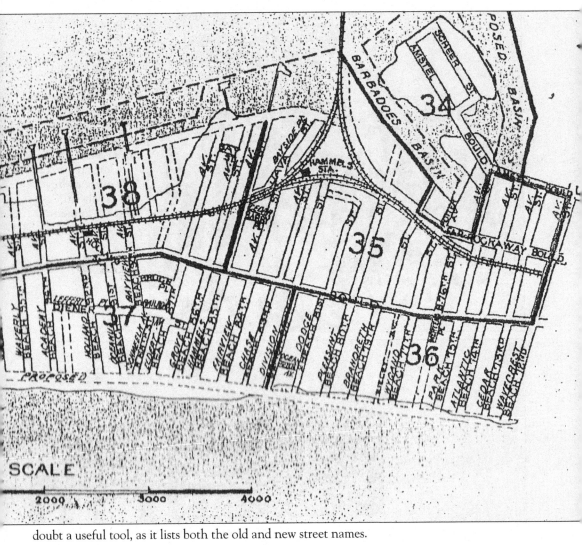

doubt a useful tool, as it lists both the old and new street names.

There was reportedly some resistance to the naming scheme, and the old street names did not begin to fade until the 1920s. The sign hanging above this construction site and crew notes the office address on Beach 116 Street, "formerly Fifth Avenue."

Pictured is another interesting sign of the times. This sign accompanies the construction of Jamaica Bay Boulevard—now known as Cross Bay Boulevard—and the Cross Bay Bridge, "largest vehicular trestle in the world" in the early 1920s. (Courtesy of Ed Gloeggler.)

The Rockaway Beach secessionists had pushed hard for the construction of a highway across Jamaica Bay connecting the community to the rest of the city. This rare early-1920s view shows equipment in place with the work in progress. (Courtesy of Edward and Dorothy Auer Sullivan.)

The original structure, which opened in 1925, was a two-lane, double lift, concrete bascule design with only 25 feet of clearance for boats and a simple circular off-ramp for cars. The bridge was later widened to four lanes and raised in 1939, so that larger boats could pass beneath it, and a more elaborate on- and off-ramp structure was added.

To adorn the approach area of the bridge, on November 12, 1927, a statue was dedicated to commemorate individuals in the community who had died serving in World War I. The monument is shown at its original location on Beach Channel Drive and Beach 95 Street, but it was later moved two blocks south to its present location on Rockaway Beach Boulevard between Beach 94 and Beach 95 Streets. (Courtesy of New York City Parks photo archive.)

Milton C. Baillie	Leland Schmeelk	John Bond, Jr.
Russel Cole	Winfield Pike	Harry Powles
Louis Davenport	William Knott	Knut Olson
Albert Davenport	John Boyle	Joseph Etter
William Baum	John C. Bell	Richard Murrell
Marshall Tucker	Lars Andersen	Emil Schwan
Walter Bossard	Warner Murray	Ida Schoncke
Dewey Smith	Charles Jones	J. C. Arnold
Raymond Kreuscher	Nelson Hewlett	Chester Rogers
Harold Smith	Charles Muck	Fred Davis
Albert Lance	William Smith	Raymond McKeown
Clinton Stoddart	Fred Schottler	Arthur Repperger
Charles L. Jacobi	Victor Agrillo	Kenneth Carpenter
Reginald Sierer	Harold George	J. Philip Nordeck
Leland Thursby	George DeGroot	Warren Jones
Hubert Murray	Frank DeGroot	Frank George
Hamilton Montgomery	Harry Schilling	Garrett Schmeelk
Richard Swain	John Farrington	Richard Roland
Robert Sickman	Edward Closs	Thomas Layer
Frank Kupper	Conrad Baum	Raymond Hensler
William Long	Ralph Dane	George Pfersching
Harry Pfister	Frank Haentschke	Edward Duncan
Albert B. Jennings	Edward Knott	Donald Appleton
Elmer Johnson	Harold Boyle	Edward George
Garrett Carman	Rowland Seaman	Chester Boyle
John Schwan	Stacey Maney	George Zimmerman
Fred. Schmidt	Gilbert George	Ira Pearsall
George Cunningham	Henry Rau	William Washelm
Fred N. Verity	Arthur Pfister	Richard Rutter
Milton Kreuscher	Foster Gunther	George Zimmermann
George C. Hough	Edwin Hough	George Edwards
Arthur Rush	Henry Washeim	Robert Carman
Frank Seelig	Albert Gilmore	Frank Gustafson
Howard Montgomery	Francis M. Ferguson	Howard Shaw
Charles Carman	George Ferguson	George Ormond
Frank Keeton	William Ferguson	George Gunther
Chester Carle	John Johnson	

When American troops were sent in 1917 to help fight World War I in Europe, 110 members of the First Congregational Church enlisted. Four died in action, including Frank George, great-grandson of Fannie Holland. Two of his brothers also served, as did John Bond Jr. and Ida Schoncke, daughter of lumber entrepreneur Henry Schoncke. Many Rockaway Beach families sent more than one child to war, as this list shows, including the Boyles, Carmans, Fergusons, Knotts, Schmeelks, and Schwans. (Courtesy of FCC.)

Prior to the construction of the bridge and the mass invasion of the automobile, the Holland Avenue Pier, now Beach 92 Street on the bay, remained one of the most important entrance points to the community. It is pictured in September 1922. (Courtesy of Len Kohn.)

Modest bay-front establishments remained popular into the 1920s, but they would soon be eclipsed by new trends in lodging. Also, the failure of the Iron Steamboat Company in 1931 during the Great Depression reduced the number of visitors arriving at these piers by ship. Hemberger's Hotel, built in 1910, has been rechristened as the Bayside Hotel in this 1932 photograph. (Courtesy of the *Wave*, Howard Santamore Collection.)

The early years of the 20th century brought a sense of solidity to permanent residents at the beach and marked the arrival of an important new innovation for summer visitors. Casual, seasonal housing in small wooden structures, known as bungalows, became popular. John J. Eagan's bungalow colony was built in 1905, and the structures were prefabricated units. (Courtesy of Edward and Dorothy Auer Sullivan.)

Even more casual were open-air tents. William Auer started a colony of tents near Beach 98 Street in 1905, after he lost the lease for an earlier effort near Beach 106 Street. During this time period, the summer population of Rockaway Beach had risen to more than 100,000. (Courtesy of the Auer family.)

To the right is a portrait of William Auer and his sister Louise around the time he established his tent colony. There were 8,000 bungalows on the peninsula by 1915. Photographs, like the one below, advertised Schilling's Seaside Bungalows at Beach 100-101 Streets and Marsell's Bay City on the bay from Beach 98-100 Streets. Bay Towers, two 14-story high-rise buildings, replaced Marsell's classic bungalow court in 1968, and a community of attached duplex homes called Belle Shores later replaced most of Schilling's. (Right, courtesy of Auer family; below, courtesy of Edward and Dorothy Auer Sullivan.)

This view shows residents seated along the interior walkway of a bungalow colony. Trees and awnings provided shade on a hot summer day. Marsell's advertising mentioned ample parking and numerous daily trains running direct to the colony from Manhattan and Brooklyn, plus "one of the largest swimming pools in the world" nearby. (Courtesy of Edward and Dorothy Auer Sullivan.)

The area featured wholesome attractions for families, although parks activists and bureaucrats from Manhattan dubbed them "cheap amusements" and derided the fact that they were privately owned. The operations were quite profitable. Midway Kiddie Park was operated by the Auer family, and later became Seaside Kiddie Land. (Courtesy of Auer family.)

Shown are two vintage photographs of the Flier (above) and Frolic (below), two rides at Midway Kiddie Park that provided regular seasonal jobs for local residents. (Both, courtesy of Auer family.)

This ride operator, pictured above in the center, was a longtime employee of the Auers. In 1922, Queens Borough president Maurice Connolly published drawings of what Rockaway Beach would look like with a wide automobile parkway along the ocean lined with elegant 14-story apartment buildings. Better roadways were a demand of the Rockaway Beach secession movement, but nobody had ever asked for high-rise housing. Connolly's vision would later be realized by Robert Moses. The city satisfied the secession movement's demand for a new boardwalk in 1929 (below), but in the process removed many of the businesses nearest the sand. (Above, courtesy of Auer family, below, courtesy of Ed Gloeggler.)

Oblivious to the planning going on to change their little resort village, the people of Rockaway Beach enjoyed the Roaring Twenties with abandon. Both social mores and bathing suits were less confining. Rose Werner (right) and her sister, Ada, proudly pose in their bathing attire. (Courtesy of Rosemary Werner Tighe.)

Rose (Krueger) Werner's family operated Krueger's Sea Beach House, near Beach 108 Street in Seaside. William Werner and his parents pose in front of the business upon his graduation in the 1920s. (Courtesy of Rosemary Werner Tighe.)

William Werner was a true scholar and athlete. He was valedictorian and captain of the basketball team at Far Rockaway High School. Werner was later top of his class and played roundball at New York University, graduating in 1927. (Courtesy of Rosemary Werner Tighe.)

The peninsula has had an enduring passion for the sport of basketball. In the 1920s, young women of Rockaway Beach participated in basketball programs in church and civic halls. These young ladies are 1928–1929 champions at St. Rose of Lima. Ruth Anthony (Bittrich) (first row, right) was later a longtime lay leader of the First Congregational Church. (Courtesy of FCC.)

Others, including local Violet Rogers (first row, second from left), participated in a team called the Long Island Lassies, which was active in the late 1920s. Games were played in various locations in the metropolitan area, and coverage was extensive in the newspapers of Brooklyn, Queens, and Long Island. (Courtesy of FCC.)

This group of local girls became champions of Queens, probably in the early 1920s. These photographs show that there was great variety in the styles of uniforms. (Courtesy of FCC.)

A 1939 Rockaway Beach football team, the White Elephants, shows various immigrant groups melding in the neighborhood. From left to right are (first row) Edward Miles, Murray Shapiro, ball boy/mascot Ralph Velardi, Nicholas Velardi, and John McKeon; (second row) Timothy O'Connor, Ken Johnston, Harry Romas, Thomas DiResta, Eli Kastenbaum, and ? Collins; (third row) Emitt Hoobs, Anthony DiResta, unidentified, Pat Von Weisenstein, Louis Cavoores, Peter Savidis, unidentified, and unidentified. (Courtesy of Marie E. Velardi.)

Swimming was the only sport to rival basketball's popularity. In the 1920s, before the City of New York took over parks operations at Rockaway Beach, Queens Borough had its own lifeguard squad. From left to right are Mike Casale, Larry Mack, George O'Connor, Jim Walsh, Joe Corrigan, Gus Paris, and Bill Ennis; in the top row is Dick Randell.

There were no basketball courts in Seaside during the Depression years, and children of working-class families were unable to afford basketballs. The famous McGuire brothers, Al and Dick, and their friends Ed Bacalles and Norman Ochs, made a basketball by wrapping rubber bands around a wad of newspaper, and hung a basket on a telephone pole. Bacalles credits Robert Moses for building the basketball court at Beach 108 Street in Seaside, near the McGuire family's bar, where a core group of players who would later form the nucleus of the National Basketball Association started playing together in the 1940s. Photographs of famous players from classic outdoor games of this era are hard to find, but this portrait of a Rockaway Nationals 1951 championship team sponsored by a local synagogue shows that the popularity of basketball cut across many cultures.

For those who preferred the arts to an athletic arena, Rockaway Beach in the 1920s and 1930s offered abundant creative outlets. The brass band of St. John's Home for Boys regularly visited the peninsula, long before the institution moved from Brooklyn to Rockaway Park in 1948. The *Wave* noted its performance at the local Christmas tree lighting ceremony in 1919, and they are shown here as the featured entertainers at the 90th Street Association Easter party in March 1937 (above). The backgrounds of these photographs show that there were still large, open stretches of land in the Holland section of Rockaway Beach at this time. (Both, courtesy of Marie E. Velardi.)

Vaudeville-type productions were staples of the community in days before television and movies became widely available. Productions occurred not just in Rockaway Beach, but in churches and social clubs in Broad Channel, Rockaway Point, and Rockaway Park. "Fairyland," a show produced by the First Congregational Church Sunday School (above), featured performers costumed as fairy-tale characters, such as these two children (below). Alfred J. Bedell joined a group called the Oceanus Dramatic League. He relates in his memoirs, "people were starved for entertainment, so it was not hard to fill up the churches, hospitals and schools." (Courtesy of FCC.)

Tom Thumb wedding pageants were inspired by a real wedding of two "little people" promoted by the P.T. Barnum Circus. The marriage of world-renowned Barnum performer Charles Sherwood Stratton ("General Tom Thumb" was his stage name) to Lavinia Warren at New York City's Trinity Church on February 10, 1863, created a media frenzy. The bride and groom were both of extremely short stature due to a condition sometimes known as dwarfism. Sunday school students were recruited to perform the roles of miniature brides, grooms, ministers, and guests for these copycat pageants. Organizers of one such 1920s extravaganza at First Congregational pose with Rev. John C. Green and his wife (above, first row, far right). The miniature "bride and groom," Corliss and George Colton, pose in their quite elaborate costumes (left). (Both, courtesy of FCC.)

The 1920s were the heyday of the flapper. The sign in front of this popular boardwalk attraction advertises "face lifting while you wait" at Miss Rockaway's Beauty Shoppe. Young women graduating from Public School 44 in 1929 (below) show the trend in their hair accessories. An unidentified African American child is in the first row to the far right. Alfred J. Bedell recalled that the first black family moved to Rockaway Beach in the early 1900s. By 1945, there were 2,500 African Americans on the peninsula. (Above, courtesy of Edward and Dorothy Auer Sullivan; below, courtesy of Auer family.)

The stock market crashed in 1929, starting the Great Depression. Pres. Franklin D. Roosevelt later described 1932 as a year of closed banks and factories, bread lines and starvation wages, foreclosures, bankruptcies, and stalled railroads. The people of Rockaway Beach lost their bank. Pictured are the classes that made their first communions in 1932 (above) and their confirmations in 1938 at St. Camillus, a Roman Catholic church established in 1908 on Rockaway Beach Boulevard at Beach 100 Street. (Below, courtesy of Edward Bacalles.)

In 1932, the First Congregational Church celebrates the 50th anniversary of its Sunday school with a reenactment of the first classes conducted in the home of Fannie Holland in the 1880s (above). Sunday school teacher Cora Babcock (left) would later endow a chair in English literature at Hartwick College with a gift of securities valued at $40,000 upon her death in 1945. On this 50th-anniversary occasion, the church also feted two surviving members of the first Sunday school class (below). Mary Ella Dodge (Sherwood) (center) and Isadora Holland (Barnes) (right) descended from two pioneering families at the beach. John Jamieson, longtime superintendent of the Sunday school, did not live to see this event. He died suddenly after contracting influenza in 1928. (Both, courtesy of FCC.)

A commemorative dinner in 1932 would be one of the last major events held in the First Congregational Church building before the congregation was uprooted to its present location on Beach 94 Street, near the Cross Bay Bridge ramps. With 800 members at the time, the church was bursting at the seams, and lay leader John Jamieson provided them with a new, large building site before his death. (Both, courtesy of FCC.)

The 50th anniversary of the church in 1936 would be celebrated in the newly built John C. Green Chapel. Today, the building is utilized for church fundraisers, rented for weddings and showers, and hosts meetings of community groups, such as Alcoholics Anonymous and Narcotics Anonymous. (Both, courtesy of FCC.)

The site where the congregation worshipped from 1899 to 1938 is now a municipal parking lot. As the building was about to be bulldozed, church member George Clark penned this verse: "Workmen, take care how you handle those stones. Those timbers and beams lay aside. And those holy windows take down piece by piece. For they were our joy and our pride." Similar nostalgia is expressed to this day about the majestic Public School 44, seen below in a 1938 photograph, which ultimately ended up facing a parking lot, then was torn down completely in the early 1960s. (Above, courtesy of Ed Gloeggler; below, courtesy of NYC Municipal Archives.)

John Jamieson dreamed of a courthouse in Rockaway Beach, and his dream finally came to fruition after his death. Dedicated in September 1932, the Rockaway courthouse at Beach 90 and Beach Channel Drive was an attractive new entrance point to the peninsula. The builders touted its design, which ensured that "all rooms have a maximum of light and air, without exposure to street noise." The building site was reclaimed from the bay with landfill, and the massive Tennessee marble structure was secured with 360 concrete piles sunk into the bedrock. Today, the building is sealed up and swathed in scaffolding to protect pedestrians from falling debris. (Above, courtesy of Ed Gloeggler; below, courtesy of Vivian R. Carter.)

The removal of many boardwalk concessions and attractions in the 1920s would be followed by a much bigger effort in 1938 and 1939, under the direction of New York City's parks commissioner Robert Moses. Seen in the white hat on the far right, Moses is talking with his entourage on a tour of Jacob Riis Park—40 blocks west of Rockaway Beach—in 1934. (Courtesy of New York City Parks photo archive.)

Moses was a staunch exercise and fitness advocate. He had been a competitive swimmer in college and was a devotee of ocean bathing throughout his lifetime. At the time when he became parks commissioner, it was said that children in Manhattan had to line up for a turn to use a sandbox; however, no such problems existed in Rockaway Beach. Pictured is a large parks department calisthenics class at Beach 97 Street in 1935. (Courtesy of New York City Parks photo archive.)

Moses saw to it that the parks department built fitness facilities for people of all ages, but he also sought to appeal to contemporary trends. This meant construction of outdoor tennis, handball, and basketball courts, playgrounds, and a popular roller rink. An aerial view facing west along the completed Shorefront Parkway in 1939 shows the extent of the recreational offerings added by Moses. Of course, some of the local businesses swept away by urban development, like the Atlantic Park Hotel, had already been hosting bike races, basketball, and track events in their outdoor and indoor facilities as early as 1899. (Courtesy of Ed Gloeggler.)

Old-timers say that the Great Depression did not impact Rockaway Beach as intensely as other communities, since it was a destination where people could escape the hard times—even for just a few hours. To people of that era, it was not just about exercise and fitness, but also a chance to stroll and smoke a nice stogie. John Livich is still smiling at his Hammels boardwalk cigar stand in 1933 (left). Livich's godson, Emil R. Lucev, was just learning to read. He and his mother, Anna, enjoy an outing on the boardwalk in Hammels in 1935 (below). (Both, courtesy of Emil R. Lucev Sr.)

Young Emil R. Lucev shows off his new toy car to friends Lawrence and Helen Santich during a 1935 ride on the boardwalk in the Hammels section. (Courtesy of Emil R. Lucev Sr.)

Scouting became very popular during the Depression. George Shirkey led this troop at the First Congregational Church. Congressman William F. Brunner chaired a fundraising campaign for local Scouts, and awards were given to an outstanding Boy Scout of each religious faith, referred to as the Catholic, Hebrew, and Protestant "Star Scouts." (Courtesy of FCC.)

Condemnation awards from the City of New York were quite favorable to some landowners. These dramatic before-and-after photographs depict the razing of an old roller coaster in Seaside during the 1930s. (Both, courtesy of Auer family.)

The tower of the Irish Circle restaurant on Beach 102 Street and the second story of the Crystal Hotel are visible to the right in the demolition photograph above. Below, a crater remains when the bulldozers have gone at Beach 96 Street, which would later adjoin Shorefront Parkway. (Above, courtesy of Edward and Dorothy Auer Sullivan; below, courtesy of Auer family.)

By 1938, William Auer's tent-rental business and kiddie concessions had been dramatically reduced in size. Just one or two rows of tents are left on the oceanfront at Beach 98 Street. (Courtesy of Auer family.)

Auer diversified, beginning to operate a popular custard stand in the late 1930s, when there were about 40,000 permanent residents on the peninsula. Many longtime residents still remember the custard stand fondly. Auer (standing) presides over a family gathering in 1935. His wife, Gloria, is seated on his left side. (Courtesy of the Auer family.)

By 1937, Robert Moses had completed the much-heralded Marine Parkway Bridge (right upper corner of photograph) and was about to build the controversial Shorefront Parkway along the ocean in Rockaway Beach. He began establishing Beach Channel Drive, a wide, new roadway along the bay, to connect Shorefront Parkway to the two bridges. The photograph above documents the extensive filling-in of shoreline areas. Cross Bay Bridge was widened and a complex on- and off-ramp structure added in 1939. As a result, a spacious garden north of the present-day First Congregational Church site (below) was dramatically reduced in size. (Both, courtesy of FCC.)

The garden had been surrounded by a rustic fence reminiscent of the area's past. An aerial view of the bridge approach (below) shows how much the ramp structure encroached on the property of the church (upper right-hand corner). The remains of the Jamieson & Bond Company's loading docks can be seen at the bay front, in the lower left corner. The bridge carried 10,000 cars a day in its first year of operations at a toll of 15¢ per car. (Above, courtesy of FCC; below, courtesy of Ed Gloeggler.)

A new sanctuary was built to replace the old church structure on the boulevard, which had been torn down. A cornerstone-laying ceremony is shown in 1941 (above). Pastor Emeritus John C. Green is at far left, and Pastor Ellsworth Richardson holds a trowel at right. A parsonage was built in 1956 to accompany the Georgian-style sanctuary (below) and to accommodate the family of the new pastor, Henry M. Childs Jr., who arrived in 1951. (Both, courtesy of FCC.)

The keys to the new church building were ceremonially handed off to Pastor Richardson by Hubert D. Murray, chair of the building committee, who was also the publisher of the *Wave* newspaper at the time. Pastor Emeritus John C. Green is at far right. (Courtesy of FCC.)

Pastor Henry M. Childs Jr. (second row, left) leads members in celebration of the 70th anniversary of the church in 1956. Descendants of original church members, from left to right, include Cora (Seaman) Sprague, Ella (Holland) George, and Adelaide (Jamieson) Rogers (far right). (Courtesy of FCC.)

By 1941, the Long Island Rail Road train tracks had been placed on an elevated structure, costing over $3 million, with a new roadway beneath. This satisfied yet another of the Rockaway secession movement's earlier demands. The newly elevated tracks, which started at Beach 108 Street and ended at Far Rockaway, are visible on the right side of this photograph of the church sanctuary under construction. (Courtesy of FCC.)

The new Holland Station was located at Beach 90 Street. Here is a view from underneath the train trestle.

An aerial view, dated about 1944, shows the entire train line on the trestle as it passes by the roller coasters of the local amusement park, Rockaway's Playland. (Courtesy of Edward and Dorothy Auer Sullivan.)

The complete panorama of bridge, parking field, train trestle, and highways can be appreciated in this aerial shot from 1939.

In 1939, the 90th Street Association—now christened the John Corrigan 90th Street Block Association—was still going strong. Corrigan, who was a local beer distributor, also served as Democratic District Leader in Rockaway.

When America sent its troops to war in 1942, women joined the workforce in greater numbers. Many women in Rockaway Beach were employed as operators at the New York Telephone Company's long-lines facility on Beach 84 Street and Rockaway Beach Boulevard, where calls were connected manually. When dial tones were instituted in the 1940s, a labor dispute resulted. Mabel Bedell holds a picket sign. (Courtesy of Lorelee Bedell.)

Even during wartime, small groups of children still made their first communions at St. Camillus, including Edward Sullivan (second row, far right). (Courtesy of Edward and Dorothy Auer Sullivan.)

During the last year of World War II, in 1945, Rockaway was hit by a huge hurricane and massive snowstorm. Dorothy Auer (Sullivan) and her sister Mary frolic outside the bungalows operated by their grandfather, many of which had been winterized for year-round residents. (Courtesy of Auer family.)

Things returned to normal after World War II ended, and fundraising activities, such as church bazaars, resumed. Homemade jams and jellies are offered by the Ladies' Aid Society of the First Congregational Church at this patriotic-themed event in 1946. (Courtesy of FCC.)

The church celebrates its 60th anniversary in 1946, paying tribute to longtime members hailing from some of the area's pioneer families, including Isadora (Holland) Barnes (first row, left) and Cora (Seaman) Sprague (first row, right). (Courtesy of FCC.)

St. Francis de Sales in nearby Belle Harbor held a grand event in September 1946 to welcome home all 450 of its members who had served in World War II. The new mayor of New York City, William O'Dwyer, lived just one block from the church when he was inaugurated in January 1946. (Courtesy of Dean Georges.)

Three

THE VILLAGE AND THE RESORT CHANGE
1950s–1960s

The years after World War II were not kind to Rockaway Beach. Authors Lawrence and Carol Kaplan call the era a "harsh transformation of an urban community." With only 51,000 permanent residents on the entire peninsula as of the 1950 census, it could hardly be considered "urban." Rather, a village that had all the advantages of the suburbs was lost (or, some would say, destroyed) beginning in the 1950s.

To new arrivals on the peninsula, it is hard to contemplate what Rockaway Beach must have been like during the summer of 1950, when the seasonal attendance figures peaked at 48 million. Many visitors to the beach in 1950 arrived by car, but a large number continued to come by boat and by the comfortable, speedy, suburban-style Long Island Rail Road (LIRR) train service. The LIRR even featured special nonstop service from Penn Station to Playland Amusement Park on summer weekends.

All of this ended when the wooden train trestle over Jamaica Bay burned down in May 1950. The timing of this disastrous event could not have been worse. It took six years to restore service, and by then, the Rockaway Beach line had become a double-fare New York City Transit line, snaking slowly through some of the poorest neighborhoods of Brooklyn. The new service got to Manhattan in twice the time it had taken on the LIRR. Ironically, civic leaders had coveted a subway line for Rockaway Beach for decades, believing that it would lead to greater prosperity. As they say, "be careful what you wish for."

In the early 1950s, ostensibly motivated by the need to house returning veterans and their families, the city was about to build thousands of new housing units across the peninsula. Notwithstanding the 1922 drawings floated by the Queens borough president, high-rise housing had not yet come to Rockaway Beach. Change was on the horizon.

By 1955, Rockaway Beach got the hulking, oversized Hammel Houses (712 units), followed in 1964 by Dayton Beach Park (1,140 units), Dayton Towers West (648 units), and Dayton Towers (1,104 units) in 1967. Then, in 1968, two 14-story buildings known as Bay Towers replaced the fabled Marsell's Court bungalow complex (across from today's Beach Channel High School campus), at Beach 100 and Beach Channel Drive.

By 1968, Rockaway Beach looked a lot like Manhattan—but it took an hour or more to actually get there.

The Corrigan Association block party was photographed in 1947 at Greenrose's Restaurant on Beach 90 Street near the elevated train tracks. The building, greatly modified, houses a storage facility today. The sign hanging above participants in the upper right-hand corner advertises Chicken in the Rough, one of the earliest and most successful fast-food concept in the world. It would later be featured on the cover of *Time* magazine and advertised in a fundraising journal. Three Chicken in the Rough outlets remain in operation today in Michigan and Canada. (Above, courtesy of Marie E. Velardi; below, courtesy of FCC.)

In the mid-1930s, after completion of the section of Beach Channel Drive between Beach 108 Street and the Cross Bay Bridge, Playland Amusement Park owner Joseph Geist reinstituted boat service to the bayside piers. By 1948, the Wilson Line's *State of Pennsylvania* was bringing passengers to the Beach 98 Street dock on a regular schedule. Other ships serviced the pier near Marsell's bungalow court, including the *Liberty Belle*, out of Yonkers, New York. The Livingston and Vasselman families prepare to board the *Liberty Belle* for a day of adventure in the 1950s. (Right, courtesy of Dotsy Livingston Kearns.)

The bungalows at Marsell's Court were always booked for the summer. Maureen Corrigan (Henning) and her mother, Mae Corrigan, pose near the family's bungalow in 1949 (above). An end-of-summer Mardi Gras event at Marsell's Court in the early 1960s (below) shows that large outdoor spaces adjacent to small family housing units were quite popular at the time. (Both, courtesy of Maureen Corrigan Henning.)

On the right is another image of friends dressed in rolled-up jeans and sailor hats inspired by World War II naval garb and having a grand time at Marsell's Court. From left to right are Pat Maggio, Theresa DeLisse, and an unidentified friend. These young men in the 1950s favored sitting on the dock at the bay (below). The Cross Bay Bridge can be seen in the background. From left to right are Bobby Page, Anthony LaRocca, and Joe Gregorio. (Both, courtesy of Betsy Lograno.)

The year 1950 was a banner year for Rockaway Beach, with a record number of summer visitors, calculated at 48 million. This was cited at the time as the largest usage of public beaches in the world. The classic view of Rockaway's Playland in about 1950 is pictured above, and a more unusual way of looking at it is pictured below. (Both, courtesy of Ed Gloeggler.)

A 1950s-era Playland beauty pageant is pictured on the right. The Playland clown logo became an icon in Rockaway, seen below. (Both, courtesy of Ed Gloeggler.)

Even on rainy days, amusements at Playland had some visitors, and police protection was required. (Courtesy of Ed Gloeggler.)

Parades were heavily attended during that era. The annual Mardi Gras parade at the close of the season passes spectators at Playland.

A 1952 Memorial Day parade includes this troop of Girl Scouts (above). Patriotism has always been in style on the peninsula. A young man in a sailor uniform marches past the Playland parking lot (right). (Both, courtesy of the *Wave* and Dan Mundy, Ed Clarity Collection.)

Catholic youth organizations, including groups for girls (above) and boys (below), have been regular participants in Rockaway Beach parades for decades. They are pictured marching in 1952. (Both, courtesy of the *Wave* and Dan Mundy, Ed Clarity Collection.)

The Daniel O'Connell American Legion
Post proudly hoists its flags in the parade
as its passes Auer's Custard Stand,
formerly located at the southwest corner
of Beach 95 Street and Rockaway Beach
Boulevard. (Courtesy of the *Wave* and
Dan Mundy, Ed Clarity Collection.)

A group of veterans marches past the
Rockaway Beach National Bank building
during the Memorial Day parade in May
1955. The signage shows that the majestic
bank building had been converted into
a bathhouse. (Courtesy of the Daniel
O'Connell American Legion Post.)

By the early 1960s, the bank building had become the Rockaway Beach Republicans' clubhouse. The St. Camillus Marching Band's Brass Ensemble struts past during yet another parade. (Courtesy of Dotsy Livingston Kearns.)

Temple Israel was built on Beach 84 Street in 1900, but the congregation went out of existence in the 1960s. Temple Beth El was founded in Rockaway Park in the early 1920s. A joint interfaith service between the temple and the First Congregational Church began in 1927 and continues to this day, with the service location alternating biannually. The temple is pictured hosting church members in 1952. (Courtesy of FCC.)

In September 1951, St. Camillus Roman Catholic Church, which had previously been considered a seasonal resort parish, opened a parochial school for children of year-round residents. Msgr. William Burke, formerly at St. Francis deSales in Belle Harbor, supervised the school from the outset, even helping children cross the street (above). Students in the inaugural classes line up outside on Beach 99 Street (below). St. Rose of Lima Roman Catholic Church on Beach 84 Street would open its own parochial school in 1966. (Below, courtesy of Dotsy Livingston Kearns.)

The year after the school was founded, Monsignor Burke put out a call for recruits to the St. Camillus Fife, Drum, and Bugle Corps. More than 500 children participated from 1952 to 1962. A performance outside Playland in the late 1950s is pictured above. In 1964, the corps is shown at the 1964 World's Fair at Flushing Meadow Park (below). Another Seaside group, the Irish-American Band (sometimes called the "American-Irish Band"), also provided a creative outlet for local teens during this era. (Both, courtesy of Dotsy Livingston Kearns.)

The two worlds of Rockaway Beach existed side by side in the mid-1950s. The tightly drilled marchers of the band are pictured standing at attention to perform at a Hammels location, while neighborhood residents on the porches of nearby tenement housing pause to watch and listen. (Courtesy of Dotsy Livingston Kearns.)

Participants gather around at a fire department civil defense program for children in the Hammels section in 1956, showing the growing ethnic diversity of the area.

In July 1952, Robert Moses would assert that much of the peninsula had become a "resort slum." The following year, he chose the Seaside section for a middle-income Title I project over the opposition of the Seaside Property Owners' Association, the chamber of commerce, and the Rockaway Beach Property Owners, who lobbied to locate the project in Hammels and won. Above, the Hammel Houses, a 712-unit project, was completed by the Zukerman organization in 1955. Many older homes, stores, and a movie theater were torn down in the demolition, including the Levine family residence on Beach 84 Street. At left, Sharon Levine (Gabriel) (first row, in the dark hat) and friends gathered on the porch with her uncle, Leo Levine, in the early 1950s. (Left, courtesy of Sharon Levine Gabriel.)

Until 1950, Rockaway families enjoyed a quick, comfortable commute on the suburban-style Long Island Rail Road trains that arrived at Manhattan's Penn Station in 30 minutes. On May 7, 1950, the trestle over Jamaica Bay burned down while the railroad was in dire financial straits. The service did not return until June 1956, at which point it had been taken over by New York City Transit. The new route traveled through some of the poorest neighborhoods in Brooklyn. Mayor Robert Wagner is pictured above holding a poster advertising the new service, and the completed line is shown in the aerial photograph below. (Both, courtesy of New York Transit Museum.)

At the close of the 1950s, despite huge changes that had occurred in terms of the peninsula's housing and transit, families of many backgrounds still mingled together in Rockaway Beach social and fraternal organizations. The Rotary International, a vibrant group at the beach that still exists today, includes members of diverse backgrounds who join together on charitable projects. They sponsor the Gift of Life Program, assist children with terminal illnesses through Ronald McDonald House, and collect for local food pantries. Here, members and their spouses attend an international convention in June 1959. John and Marie Kimball of Neponsit are the fourth and fifth from the front in the far-left table row, and Dr. William Werner is fourth from the front in the left row of the table on the right. (Courtesy of Dean Georges.)

Bowling leagues retained their popularity in the late 1950s. Dr. William Werner (center, holding bowling ball) was a champion bowler for the Rockaway Rotary team. (Above, courtesy of Dean Georges; below, courtesy of Rosemary Werner Tighe.)

The Knights of Columbus, a Catholic fraternal service organization for men founded at St. Camillus in the 1920s, broke ground for its chapter headquarters on Beach 90 Street in 1958. Msgr. William Burke blesses the event, while Matt Kennedy wields a shovel. Looking on from left to right are Otto Jurgens, Harold Ferguson, and John "Jackie" Keough. (Courtesy of Rockaway Knights of Columbus.)

As the 1960s began, Rockaway Beach endured major changes. The Rockaway Beach Hospital bore a "for sale" sign after the new Peninsula Hospital Center in Arverne opened. As this book went to press, the future survival of Peninsula Hospital was in question.

The old, but classic, Public School 44 was demolished (above) after the new Public School 183 had been built on Beach 79 Street. Blocks and blocks of land along Shorefront Parkway were likewise scraped clean of older buildings, to be replaced by a series of Mitchell-Lama high-rise cooperative apartment buildings (below). (Both, courtesy of the *Wave*, Howard Santamore Collection.)

The Mitchell-Lama high-rise cooperative buildings along Shorefront Parkway can be seen in the background in this 1997 photograph of the train trestle. The darker-brick Hammels projects can be seen in the foreground. The Rockaway Beach Hospital is the bulky structure located between the trestle and the bay, as the train track rounds the bend to the right. (Courtesy of New York Transit Museum.)

By the 1960s, St. Camillus occupied almost an entire block. The bungalows with dark roofs in the upper right-hand corner of the photograph were largely replaced much later by the Belle Shores development, which consisted of attached, single-family homes. A small group of bungalows remains at that location today. (Courtesy of Dotsy Livingston Kearns.)

Four

CAN SUCCESS
BE RECAPTURED?
1970s–2012

According to the 1970 census, the permanent population of the Rockaway Peninsula had risen to over 73,000, more than double the number recorded in 1930. The summer-resident population, however, had practically disappeared, due to the closing of virtually all the hotels and bungalow colonies. Because day-trips to Rockaway Beach were more arduous on the subway than they had been on the LIRR, there were also fewer day visitors.

Residents began to notice that high-rise housing was not the only change in the neighborhood. As the resort declined, many older buildings were being deployed as social welfare facilities. The Rockaway Beach Hospital was put up for sale in the early 1960s after the new Peninsula Hospital Center opened in Arverne, and the building later became a controversial drug rehabilitation facility. The Rockaway Beach National Bank building was torn down to build Surfside Manor, another controversial social services facility. The Rockaway courthouse, a splendid, classical Greek-style structure clad in Tennessee marble, was only 30 years old when the city decided to mothball it in 1962. As of this writing, plans for another health-related facility are being proposed for that site, while the building slowly crumbles.

Playland Amusement Park closed in the mid-1980s. Desirable, low-rise housing was built on the site, but many miss the summer entertainment that Playland provided.

Surfing is undergoing a huge resurgence of popularity, and there are more bicyclists visiting the peninsula as well. The types of healthy meals that surfers, bicyclists, and other young visitors crave have been the talk of print and electronic media for the past summer season or two. Casual, open-air snack stands hearken back to the days of Aunt Abby's clam chowder house in the 1850s.

Meanwhile, residents lobby for improved transportation, recreation, and schools. Business district improvement is also high on the agenda of concerns. Many hope that Rockaway Beach will again become a wildly popular resort, and that its prosperity will be shared by all. They also strive to understand why social services operations continue to find the peninsula more attractive than retail and tourism businesses, and elected officials seem unable to reverse the trend. New forms of civic involvement, including a local experiment called the "participatory budgeting process," are on the horizon. It is hoped that this will also spur positive, long-lasting change.

Surf culture first entered the mainstream in the United States during the early 1960s, but a core group of surfing fans had existed in Rockaway Beach somewhat earlier. Just like the local basketball pioneers, with their wads of newspaper wrapped up in rubber bands, the first local surfers borrowed ironing boards from their mothers to ride waves. One of the best was Dee McLean, pictured in 1966. He got an endorsement contract with Hobie in 1965. (Courtesy of Steve Stathis.)

Another Rockaway Beach surfer, Pat Reen, was arrested at Beach 91 Street in the early 1960s for using an "unauthorized flotation device." The Rockaway Surfing Club was formed, and the group went to city hall in 1967 wearing club jackets to lobby for better recognition of the sport. Club member Steve Stathis, holding newspaper, is pictured with friends and their surfboards near the boardwalk in the 1960s. (Courtesy of Steve Stathis.)

By 1965, surfing magazines had written about Rockaway Beach, and some of the local surfers were able to afford real longboards, which were made at a surf shop in Jamaica, Queens. Dee McLean is pictured riding a longboard. A few local entrepreneurs even began making their own surfboards in a storefront on Rockaway Beach Boulevard near Beach 112 Street. John Hannon began building surfboards in the city in 1964. He visited Rockaway Beach in August 1970, and was joined by a group of teens for a surfing demonstration (below). (Above, courtesy of Steve Stathis; right, courtesy of New York City Parks photo archive.)

Dennis McLean, Dee's brother, was also a top surfer. He catches waves in these c. 1973 photographs. Some speculate that surfing waned in popularity when Vietnam changed the national mood in the early 1970s. Nonetheless, locals continued to surf, and by lobbying elected representatives, they finally secured a change in state health laws, which had prohibited bathing and surfing on the same beaches. In 2005, the first surfing-only beach in New York City was established at Beach 86 Street, followed by a later designation of Beach 92 Street as well. (Both, courtesy of Steve Stathis.)

Regular boat service to Rockaway Beach had ceased by the 1970s, and most visitors during that era arrived by subway or private automobile. In 1970, the Cross Bay Bridge got a much-needed renovation, and Gov. Nelson Rockefeller helped dedicate it. The St. Camillus Marching Band appeared at the ceremony. Here, Dotsy Livingston (Kearns) greets Governor Rockefeller, as Mary Jane Judge (Tufano) stands at attention. (Courtesy of Dotsy Livingston Kearns.)

Mayor John Lindsay (far left) is pictured in 1969 after he arrived to inspect beach replenishment that occurred after severe storms had eroded a large part of the beach and boardwalk. A budget crisis gripped the city in the 1970s. The Peninsula Branch Library was due to be built at the old Public School 44 site, with funds allocated during Mayor Wagner's term; however, Lindsay cut the budget, so only a spare, utilitarian library building was constructed in 1971. (Courtesy of New York City Parks photo archive.)

The Wave Publishing Company moved several times over the years before arriving at its present location at 88-08 Rockaway Beach Boulevard. In 1977, publisher Leon Locke (far right) hosts a ribbon-cutting ceremony at 92-05 Rockaway Beach Boulevard, with clippers wielded by New York City councilman Walter Ward (center, in hat). Len and Marilyn Kohn are at far left. (Courtesy of Len Kohn.)

As the 1970s and 1980s progressed, Playland Amusement Park continued to operate, but fewer tourists came. The nearby Rockaway Beach National Bank, which had sadly been used as a bathhouse in the 1950s, was finally demolished in 1973. Attempts to reintroduce old traditions of the past, such as the beauty pageants of the 1950s, did not catch on. Pageant participants in 1974 gather around organizer Mario Russo, pictured in the jacket and tie. (Courtesy of Ed Gloeggler.)

Insurance costs forced the Geist family, who owned Playland, to consider closing the park; it actually happened in 1985. Bulldozers are pictured doing their cruel work. A development of semi-detached, duplex homes was later built on the site.

Some items of Playland memorabilia were preserved afterwards inside the offices of the Wave Publishing Company. The Rockaway Museum was formed, and initial funding was obtained from New York City Council member Al Stabile, pictured in the white shirt. Organizers pictured are, from left to right, Harold Cornell, Barbara Eisenstadt, Doris Moss, council member Stabile, and Daniel Tubridy. The museum's efforts have waned since its promising start.

By 1970, there were virtually no hotels or other housing for summer visitors to the peninsula. Decrepit bungalows in Arverne were bulldozed en masse in October 1971. Local activists, pictured at city hall, protested the numerous social welfare facilities being sited in Rockaway, such as Surfside Manor, a high-rise care facility proposed for the old Rockaway Beach National Bank site. John Jamieson would not have approved, and neither did residents, but city agencies gave their go-ahead.

Today, Rockaway Beach businesses hope to attract visitors through parks department beach programs, skateboard parks and playgrounds, and sporting events. The Rockaway Rotary has sponsored an annual running race that attracted thousands in the 1980s. The novelty wore off, and although the annual race continues, only a few hundred runners now participate.

Art exhibitions, festivals, and concerts organized by the Rockaway Music and Arts Council (RMAC) were very popular in the 1980s and 1990s. Bill Fogé, a local artist, is pictured painting St. Camillus Church. Fogé and other local artists produced original note cards and framed prints of Rockaway Beach scenes, selling them in local gift shops and during the outdoor arts festival, which was held annually each September by the RMAC from the 1980s through 2009.

In 1994, Patrick Clark, a local stained-glass artist with a studio in Rockaway Beach, incorporated the Rockaway Artists Alliance. Today, it has evolved into an educational group with galleries for exhibitions and a working artist space at the Gateway National Recreation Area, which is located west of Rockaway Beach. Gateway's historic Post Theater was renovated by the local Rockaway Theatre Company as a venue for live theatrical performances as well.

The community also hopes to attract new resident families to Rockaway Beach by supporting sports leagues, such as the Rockaway Little League, Rockaway Beach Volleyball League, Catholic Youth Organization basketball and swimming programs, and the Rockaway Rockies Hockey Club. In 1996, the parks department partnered with the Rockies to renovate the basketball court at Beach 108 Street for a new roller hockey rink. Community Board 14 District Manager Jonathan Gaska, left, pays a visit to the rink, with New York State Assembly member Audrey Pheffer, center.

In the waning years of the 1980s, one of the future trends in popular sport had a brief spate of publicity. At the urging of the Association of North Atlantic Kayakers, Gateway National Recreation Area decided to permit cartop boating, free of charge, at nearby Floyd Bennett Field. From left to right are Christina Forbes; Richard Lewitz; Don Betts; Gateway's general superintendent, Robert McIntosh Jr. (holding sign); Charles Sutherland; Janice Lozano; Andrew Singer; William Lozano; and Gateway's deputy superintendent, Larry May.

It took two more decades, but in 2010, legal launching of kayaks out of Rockaway Beach was also inaugurated at the city's newest park at Beach 88 Street, near the landing site of the original pioneers to the shore. Rockaway Parks administrator Jill Weber, with paddle, is joined by, from left to right, local human-powered boating enthusiasts Rick Horan, Vivian Carter, John Wright and Tony Pignatello (past and present Commodores, Sebago Canoe Club), and Rockaway Beach resident Roberto Rodriguez.

The popularity of surfing blossomed after the surfing beaches were dedicated. In 2008, perhaps prompted by a *New York Times* front-page feature story on the benefits of business networking on surfboards, social media types were spreading the word on the Internet that Rockaway Beach was a great place to go for a respite from the city's heat—even if it took over an hour to get there by subway. (Courtesy of the *Wave* and Denis MacRae.)

In a return to the days when simple clam chowder houses were the biggest draw in Rockaway Beach, a group of simple, seasonal food stands providing casual, tasty snacks for surfers and other hip young visitors garnered major print and electronic publicity in 2008. It is rumored that local residents enjoy the fresh-fruit ices and fish tacos as well. And there's that lone bicycle again! (Courtesy of Vivian R. Carter.)

BIBLIOGRAPHY

Bellot, Alfred H. *History of the Rockaways from the Year 1685 to 1917.* Far Rockaway, NY: Bellot's Histories, Inc., 1917.

Hendrick, Daniel M. *Jamaica Bay.* Charleston, SC: Arcadia Publishing, 2006.

History of the Rockaways. Far Rockaway, NY: Far Rockaway High School and the Exchange Club of Far Rockaway, 1932.

Kaplan, Lawrence and Carol P. Kaplan. *Between Ocean and City: The Transformation of Rockaway, New York.* New York: Columbia University Press, 2003.

Krieg, Joann P. and Natalie A. Naylor. *Nassau County: From Rural Hinterland to Suburban Metropolis.* Interlaken, NY: Empire State Books, 2000.

Lucev, Emil R. Sr. *The Rockaways.* Charleston, SC: Arcadia Publishing, 2007.

Peterson, Jon A. and Vincent Seyfried. *A Research Guide to the History of the Borough of Queens.* Jamaica, NY: Department of History, Queens College, City University of New York, 1987.

Queens Jewels: A History of Queens Parks. New York: City of New York Parks and Recreation Department, 2002.

Rockaway Review. vols. 1–32. Far Rockaway, NY: Chamber of Commerce of the Rockaways, 1935–1966.

Seyfried, Vincent and William Asadorian. *Old Rockaway, New York in Early Photographs.* Mineola, NY: Dover Publications, 2000.

St. Clair, Augustus. *Guide to Rockaway Beach and Progress of Popular Favor to the Sea.* New York: Garland & Co., 1881.

Wave. Rockaway Beach, NY: Wave Publishing Company, 1893–present.

Wave: 100th Anniversary Collector's Edition. Rockaway Beach, NY: Wave Publishing Company, 1993.

Visit us at
arcadiapublishing.com

· ·

CPSIA information can be obtained
at www.ICGtesting.com
Printed in the USA
LVOW04*0419290817

546663LV00018B/622/P